A THOMASON SKETCHBOOK

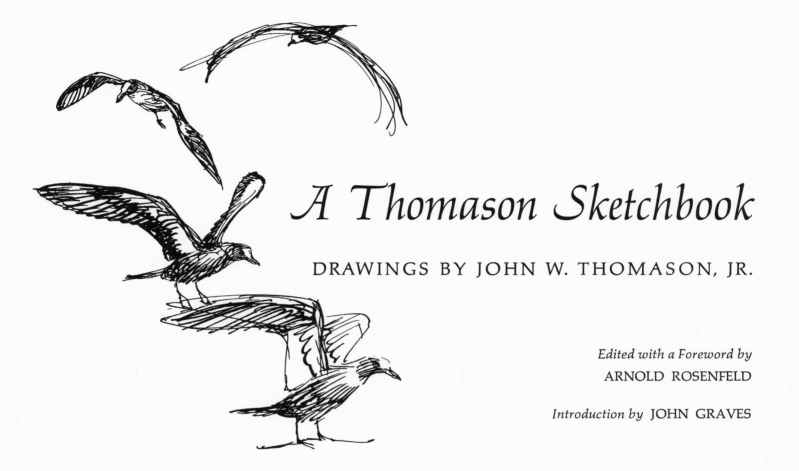

A Thomason Sketchbook

DRAWINGS BY JOHN W. THOMASON, JR.

Edited with a Foreword by
ARNOLD ROSENFELD

Introduction by JOHN GRAVES

UNIVERSITY OF TEXAS PRESS • AUSTIN AND LONDON

Standard Book Number 292-78414-7
Library of Congress Catalogue Card No. 69-13711
Copyright © 1969 by Mrs. John W. Thomason, Jr.
All Rights Reserved
Typesetting by Service Typographers, Indianapolis, Indiana
Printed by the Steck Company, Austin, Texas
Bound by Universal Bookbindery, Inc., San Antonio, Texas

FOREWORD

ONCE, involved in some of the early work on this book, I happened to ask a friend how it was that John W. Thomason, Jr., sitting in some far-off marine post in Central America or China, could draw with the utmost fidelity a soldier of a now-ancient war down to the very last curl of martial braid on his sleeve.

"If you knew Huntsville," my friend said, with what I took to be a knowledgeable smile, "you wouldn't have to ask that question." John Thomason also answered the question, but in another way, his own. In the first paragraphs of his biography of Jeb Stuart, Thomason wrote:

I sat at the feet of our old men who fought in our War of the Southern Confederacy and asked them the questions that boys ask: "What did Stonewall Jackson look like? What sort of man was Longstreet—A. P. Hill? . . ."

"Well son"—after deep thought—"Old Stonewall looked —looked—he looked like his pictures. You've seen his pictures. Longstreet, he was a thick-set sort of fellow, with a bushy beard. A. P. Hill was red-headed . . ." But when you ask about Jeb Stuart, their eyes light up and their faces quicken, and they describe details of his dress, his fighting jacket and his plume—and they hum you songs he loved and tell you how his voice sounded.

John William Thomason, Jr., was born on February 28, 1893, the son of Dr. and Mrs. John W. Thomason of Huntsville, Texas. The "War of the Southern Confederacy" was less than thirty years in the past. Huntsville was still alive with the sights and sounds of that war.

Although on a highway map Huntsville is now only a little more than an hour's drive north of Houston, it is a great distance away. The two cities are connected by a huge highway that permits the driver to make the trip without stops, in modern mindlessness, without noticing the pines the road builders have spared or how far he has actually come, not necessarily in miles but in mind. It may be that the day will come when Huntsville and Houston, spreading in the inevitable amoeba-like movements of cities, will coalesce and become indistinguishable. But for now they are still different worlds.

Houston is, briefly, a modern big city, and big cities have much in common. Its people increasingly speak the language of the cities. Its downtown area is increasingly crowded with boxlike office buildings scarcely different from those built in any other large city. Its suburbs, orderly and neat, are dotted with shopping centers, new movie theaters, and franchised restaurants, America's best testimony to the universality of man. Houston, like other big cities, appears at times to be acting out Lewis Mumford's acute observation that what every American hopes for is to travel far to find at the end of the journey that things are pretty much the same as they were at home.

Perhaps symbolically, the highway connecting the two places curves discreetly away from Huntsville, a

Texas city but, like John Thomason's work, more
Southern than Southwestern. There are some cities that
convey no sense of place, being merely conveniences
for living. Huntsville is not one of them. What Huntsville is you can feel merely by turning off the highway,
by walking along its streets. The people here have deep
roots, and history is no abstraction. Who you are has
meaning, and it is not without significance that in John
Thomason's listing in one of the standard biographical
reference works it is carefully noted that his mother,
Sue, was a Goree, and his grandmother, Emily, was an
Alabama Fisher.

In a sense, John Thomason never really left Huntsville. His work, the sketches he did in the privacy of
his imagination, are alive with Huntsville and his boyhood there. If, however, a small part of Thomason
never left Huntsville, Thomason the man did leave—
at a very early age and for a very long time.

The odyssey began in 1909 when Thomason went
off to Southwestern University at Georgetown, Texas,
to study. In the context of what was to follow, it was a
tentative journey, a boy getting his sea legs. In 1910
Thomason returned to study at the Sam Houston Nor-
mal Institute (now Sam Houston State College, where
a building is named for him). In 1912 and 1913 he
studied at The University of Texas.

If in every man's life there are turning points, one of
Thomason's must have come in 1913 when he left
Texas to go to New York City to study at the Art Stu-
dents League. He stayed two years. The sketches of his
boyhood are preserved, and although they are remarkable for their promise, they are still static and carefully
amateur. It was only after Thomason left New York for

Texas in 1915 that his drawings began to show life and movement.

After 1917 Thomason returned only when the demands of duty and his professional life—military and literary—would permit. He worked for a while for the Houston *Chronicle*, where he learned the reporter's craft, then joined the Marine Corps in 1917, was commissioned, and went to France with the Second Division. Thomason fought at Belleau Wood, at Château-Thierry, at Saint-Mihiel, and in the Meuse-Argonne campaign. He won the Navy Cross at Soissons in 1918 for taking out a German machine gun nest.

Thomason's service career after the war is the straightforward story of a professional soldier. He served with the Marines at sea, in the West Indies, in Central America, in China, and, toward the end, in the Pacific. He would lead an American landing party ashore in Nicaragua, command a company and serve as adjutant in the American legation guard in Peiping, observe the Japanese invasion of China, study at the Army and Navy War Colleges, serve as chief of the Navy Department's American Republics section, and serve on the staff of the Pacific fleet commander, Admiral Chester Nimitz.

If all this sounds like a fairly complete career for any one man, it should be recalled that Thomason at the same time was engaged in an equally full literary and artistic career. It started in 1926, when, under the urging of the late Laurence Stallings and the editorship of the fabled Maxwell Perkins of Scribner's, Thomason published his first book, *Fix Bayonets!* The book got high marks from the critics. James Norman Hall thought it ranked as a soldier's narrative with John

Masefield's *Gallipoli*. The London *Times* cheered: "No book which we can recall that has for subject the actual fighting man in the Great War, has appeared to us to equal this. The drawings match the prose."

Fix Bayonets! was followed in 1927 by *Red Pants and Other Stories*, the first of several books in which Thomason almost singlehandedly cast the image of the Marine Corps between the wars; *Marines and Others* in 1927; *Jeb Stuart* in 1930; *Salt Winds and Gobi Dust* in 1934; *Gone to Texas*, his first novel, in 1937; and *Lone Star Preacher* in 1941. In 1935 Thomason edited the *Adventures of General Marbot*. A collection of his short stories, *—And a Few Marines*, appeared in 1943. He illustrated each book, as he did most of the innumerable short stories and articles he produced for major magazines during the period.

Thomason died on March 12, 1944, at the San Diego, California, Naval Hospital. He had been serving with the Amphibious Training Command of the Pacific Fleet and was 51 at the time of his death.

At the outset the purposes of this book were fairly simple: to provide an appropriate reminder of an exceptional man to those who already knew him and to introduce him to a later generation. That was before John Thomason took a hand in the work. Most of the drawings have never been previously published. Most were never meant for publication, being the random sketches of a man whose hand could not resist setting down what his keen eye had observed. To go through the Thomason collection at Sam Houston State College (Time flies. It was Sam Houston State Teachers College

when most of the work on this book was done) and to attempt to select a fairly limited number of pictures is to know the heights of combined joy and frustration.

First the joy: Looking through the collection is a work of discovery. After a while one gets to know John Thomason and the variety of his mind. You know, for instance, that memories of home drift across these pages in the form of unnumbered ducks frozen in perfect flight. Many of the pictures contain small delightful surprises that reveal themselves only after closer examination: a tiny sketch of a horse, a small, expressive face, a fragment of motion. Thomason's eye for action was, I think, exceptional. When a Thomason horse moves, you know exactly how fast it is moving. When the proprietor of a Caribbean cabaret stands at the entrance of his establishment, you sense his greed. When a sketch captures a mood, it is that mood and no other. These are the sketches of a man who understood and was able to communicate that understanding.

The frustrations: Thomason was no worshiper at his own shrine. He discarded or gave away much of his sketchwork and completed work. He apparently regarded his sketches merely as the raw material from which a small snip of blank paper could be mined for yet another sketch. Most of the pictures in this book had, in their original form, perfectly usable sketches on the reverse side. Many of these have been used.

Some sketches are on fragments of pages, ripped from other pages long lost. Other pages contain lovely drawings torn apart when the artist, who must have been one of the great paper conservationists of our era, needed a new scrap to draw one. There is, in fact, a story that Mrs. Thomason tells of a frustrated magazine editor who wrote her, somewhat desperately I now feel assured in saying, that the next time the Colonel ran out of paper she should write immediately and the editor would forward same immediately.

Thomason drew almost constantly, and a day rarely passed when he did not draw something. He drew on his own stationery, on Marine Corps stationery, on War College stationery, on the stationery of the Commander in Chief of the United States Pacific Fleet, on the stationery of the Plebiscitary Commission of the Tacna-Arica Arbitration, on flimsy pads, on pieces of ledgers, on canvas board, and on odd and curious scraps of paper. Apparently no scrap of paper, if usable, was safe. The careful investigator will find guard rosters, military memoranda, and other indications of what Thomason always said was his principal trade.

In one sketchbook there is a wry and lively series of notes on a fox hunt he was once invited to. In the back of another there is a little dictionary of dice expressions and a series of nautical problems:

"You are officer of the deck in a heavy fog: You hear 1 long blast and 2 short whistles directly ahead: you have been hearing it for some time." Thomason's answer to the problem: "Jump overboard."

The sketches inadvertently reveal much of the man—what he was thinking, how he worked. I think it is fair to say that much of the sketchwork presented here shows what was good in John Thomason. In much but not all of his published work Thomason seemed to be working toward the publication ideal of illustration of his time—the gleam in the eye of the art editor of the *Saturday Evening Post*, for whom he did much work. He was better, much better, than that. Frequently he

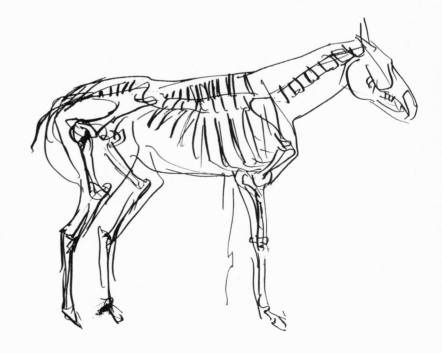

worked out an idea—and he worked hard on a drawing —with the result that the finished product contained less than the first few lines set to paper. So although Thomason knew anatomy and would repeat a detail— a hand, for example—until he had it right, some of the best work is often to be seen in a small, spontaneous sketch he did to enliven a page. Such work shows a rare freedom and simplicity of line. There are several sketches which, with one line fewer, would have ceased to exist.

His range was great. An examination of the folders in the Huntsville collection reveals finished work for publication, preliminary sketches, sketches that repeat certain themes in his work, sketches of knights in armor, gangsters of the Roaring Twenties, showgirls, fish, acrobats, boys, dogs, life drawings, landscapes, boxers, football players, polo scenes, illustrations from books and magazines, figures of the Colonial period, characters from Rider Haggard novels, Scotch clansmen, Latin-American peasants, and strange figures from the Orient and the *Arabian Nights*. And always, weaving their way in and out of exotic and varied landscapes, the birds and wildlife of home. To be set amid all this richness and to be asked to choose only relatively little is to know frustrations that would have made the labors of Sisyphus seem the height of human fulfillment. Thomason worked in a variety of media, and the works in this book range from ink to wash to watercolor.

The drawings collected here were chosen mainly to show Thomason's range and some of his vision. He was an unusual man, sensitive, tirelessly observant, witty, compassionate, and—heaven help us, for it is a word in small favor—*romantic*. There are as many equally fine pictures remaining in the collection. I hope they can be brought to light at some future date in a more complete publication.

There are a number of persons to whom I am grateful for the contributions of their time and efforts. They are Mrs. Leda Thomason of Terrell, Texas, who unhesitatingly gave permission for the use of her late husband's drawings and who has shown a continuing and valuable interest in this project; Dr. Donald Hendricks, Director of Libraries, Sam Houston State College, and Miss Aline Law, who has since retired as librarian of the Joseph L. Clark Texas Collection at the Estill Library at Sam Houston State, both of whom gave much time and co-operation to this work; and Mr. Gaddis Geeslin, dean of the School of Fine Arts and professor of arts at Sam Houston State, whose advice and help was the foundation on which this book was built. Charles Scribner's Sons of New York, Thomason's publisher, has kindly given permission to use selections from *Fix Bayonets!* and *Lone Star Preacher*. The *Saturday Evening Post* has consented to the reproduction of a sketch Thomason made for one of his articles.

Only one thing remains to be said: This is John Thomason's book, although he could have never foreseen its publication. He worked long hours sketching, revising, forging this book. His hand and mind have not been stilled by time.

ARNOLD ROSENFELD

THE OLD BREED

A note on John W. Thomason, Jr.

by John Graves

ALL of us carry, stuck inside, a good many lingering, jumbled emotional responses dating from childhood and youth that often make life richer or sweeter or more of a burden, and just as often get in the way of clear judgment. Some are solid enough to build a philosophy on, others only sentimental or angry, and it is not always easy to know the difference. Hence a man's feel for certain human attitudes and dialects and pursuits, for specific landscapes and smells and wild sounds and winds and kinds of water, is not likely to be very cool and objective even after he has been much away from them and has exercised his senses on other places and other kinds of people. Nor is he any more likely to be crisply clearheaded about certain writing, pictures, and music.

For me the stories and drawings of John W. Thomason, Jr., lie mainly within this hazy difficult realm of judgment. I first knew them young, as a Texas boy of more or less Confederate antecedents, and furthermore as one fated, maybe partly through the Thomason sto-

Portrait of John Thomason as a young officer. Drawn in 1921 by an unidentified artist.

ries and drawings themselves, to spend a war among United States Marines. The sort of recognition of yourself that you attain, especially young but later too if you stay open, out of the work of men and women who have aptly defined some of the things that you are, is more than recognition. Such work illuminates you, but it shapes you further too, and becomes a part of you. It does not have to be great to do this, but only "right" for you, and I think that ever afterward your evaluation of it is going to be somewhat suspect, whether or not you have developed further and in directions different from those early ones.

I never met Colonel Thomason, though I have a feeling that I knew him, not only through the work—a good enough avenue, for that matter—but in other ways as well that were common enough in the provincial Texas of a few years back, and in the provincial Marine Corps too. In small worlds, people tell you about other people, and most about the remarkable ones. I grew up around relatives and old friends of the Colonel's, and my mother once went to school with him, where she remembers him penciling sketch after sketch against the professorial droning from the head of the room. During the war I had a battalion commander—a friend of Thomason's and, like him, one of those improbable combinations of sensitive intelligence and masculine force that the Corps sometimes attracts— who took pride in an ability to match the literary Colonel glass for glass during long discursive weekends at San Diego. The same ability later played hell with my battalion commander's insides, but that story does not go here.

Some of the long-time officers and N.C.O.'s I knew

—the "Old Breed"—had served with Thomason at one station or another in the States or on shipboard or in the banana latitudes or troubled China during those twilight decades of old-style white man's imperialism between the big wars, when the small and solidly professional Corps, honed in France, played a busy part in upholding the American end of things as then defined. The Old Breed had studied him too, for in their legendary and leathery world he stood out as something of a legend himself, albeit one of a slightly maverick flavor, puzzling to many of the Old Breed and infuriating to a few.

I know little about the ways in which Thomason's artistic pursuits, his career as an officer, and high-level internal Marine Corps politics interreacted during the twenty-seven years he served before his untimely death in 1944, except that they did. A search for meaning and expression pulls a man toward one way of existence, one set of rules, and the emphatic extrovert leadership of men pulls him toward another, and clearly enough Thomason did not always manage to fit the two ways comfortably together, either in practical terms or within himself. Nor is it probable that all superior officers were uniformly pleased with the satiric perception of human pomp and error and flimflam that peeks through in some of his work, or with the considerable sums of extra cash it brought him during what were generally lean times for the military. You can still find retired senior officers, good marines in their time, who go frosty or vague if you mention the Colonel's name to them; I met one just a year or so ago. But you can find others who beam at such mention and start telling you stories about the man.

At this point in time, when Belleau Wood and the Somme and the Legation Guard passing in review under the Tartar Wall at old Peking have receded into our ancient history, Thomason's military career matters principally because it reflected itself strongly in the work he left behind. It is, in fact, the basis for much of that work's distinctiveness. Although as military men go he seems to have been of the eccentrically human rather than the Prussian persuasion—noted for refusing or not being able to keep step with the music in parades, addicted to certain bohemianisms in his uniform, and so on—he was nevertheless a professional, proved staunch. Possible internal conflicts notwithstanding, the tough-minded values of career soldiering are implicit in most of his stories and pictures. By and large, it is not a very articulate profession, and Thomason is one of a small handful of creative people in modern times who have been able to set down something of what soldiering means to those who follow it as a way of life, in contrast to those others of us who don a uniform and an attitude martial or otherwise for a year or two or three of crisis, and those who look at the whole military complex of things from outside with humanitarian dismay or rage.

Besides being a soldier, Thomason was a Texan, of another Old Breed, rooted in an unhomogenized time when the places where men grew up, far more than in the flexible present, put a stamp on them for better or worse that they wore through life. The pre-1914 Texas in which he reached maturity was more different from the Texas we know now than many people in large hats want to admit—barely out of its rough heroic age, agrarian, beginning to move toward twentieth-century ways but little affected yet by petroleum or industry or big money or even the modern sanctimony of the marketplace, short on boaster-boosterism, fragmented into regions whose human ways were as distinct from one another as their terrain and vegetation.

Much of it was intensely Southern and restrospective in outlook, including the southeastern part that produced Thomason. The still-vigorous Confederate patriarchs dreaming aloud over the critical clash of civilizations in which they had lost so long before and the listening young envious of them, the Old Testamental metaphysics and rhetoric, the rituals of cotton and corn and furrowbound mules, the hunting and fishing and dogs and horses, the problematic mass of Negroes still mortared into place at the base of the social pyramid, and the rest. . . Like most of the newer South before the myths got out of hand, it looked back to antebellum times characterized somewhat less by magnolias and classic porticoes than by a sense of destiny and stout log houses, and the social stratification among its whites was comfortably loose, but it was none the less Southern for all of that.

It was an organic world, ancient in its rhythms, enduring on far past its own quite definite defeat in war. It was also an imperfect world, certainly, though now that the mortared social pyramid has crumbled and large fragments of it are whizzing about our ears, we sometimes indulge ourselves in simplistic magnification of the former South's defects that neither the array of known facts nor the state of our own perfection appears to warrant. Whatever one's opinion of that

world, it had staying power, and it put out a good many strong and thoughtful people with its stamp on them, of whom John Thomason was one.

He came from its fortunate upper layers, his father and his grandfather doctors in a good town, the family of impeccably Confederate and Methodist and land-owning background. The tradition was literate, re-gional, martial, and patrician, and he lived by what he saw as its better tenets—a good soldier, an apt hand with firearms and animals and the ways of wild things, a scholar, a teller of fine wry tales over pipes and whiskey, a gentleman and a gentle man toward those whom the imperfect world of his birth and the United States Marine Corps placed subordinate to him. The whole tenor of his life, despite the fact that he moved in twentieth-century literary circles and elsewhere with aplomb and comprehension, was thus by present defini-tion somewhat archaic. It was conservative, too, though I think he would find little common cause with many of those who so denominate themselves today.

If Thomason had been only these things, he would probably have developed and functioned well and died as just another of the multitude of Rebels, born too late for Sharpsburg and the Wilderness, who during about three-quarters of a century sought and found an outlet for their martial frustration in the country's armed forces. (At San Diego when I went there in '41, one of the pieces the big band used to play for morning drill on the broad long parade ground was "Dixie," the sixty-three man boot platoons whamming out its beat with iron heels, and maybe a third of the shaven-headed recruits abrim with its connotations. . .)

But he was something else besides, and that something else denied him the contentment of being simply a first-rate officer with a Navy Cross earned at Soissons, and a Texan of solid background. It condemned him instead not only to thought and wonderment over the things that he was, and how he had come to be them, and what they meant, but also to a lifelong effort to express them in pictures and in prose. He made a good many excursions into other realms of interest, most notably in the ruminative, sometimes quirksome essays he wrote ostensibly as book reviews for H. L. Mencken's old *American Mercury*, during the years he served as literary editor of that periodical. But in most of his central work, one or the other of the Old Breed things that he was, a man of arms and a Texas Southerner, looms as a main concern. In what is probably the best of that work—certainly the best of the writing—they blend and become a single meaningful thing, as they did in Thomason himself.

You can run through his published books—which contain, I imagine, the bulk of the magazine pieces that he wanted preserved—in a few evenings' reading that will give you the full feel of his graphic talent as well, for he illustrated them himself, and so integrated with each other are texts and drawings that it is hard to think about his writing as a separate thing. *Fix Bayonets!, Red Pants and Other Stories, Marines and Others, Jeb Stuart, Salt Winds and Gobi Dust, Gone to Texas, Lone Star Preacher,—And a Few Marines.* Those are the lot, though it is worthwhile also to search out those of his drawings published as illustrations for other people's books—among them *Adventures of General Marbot*, an autobiographical saga of Na-

poleonic vintage that Thomason resurrected, edited, and handsomely adorned.

His star is in eclipse now. A majority of literate non-Texans respond to mention of him with foggy recollection or none at all, as do many Texans and probably most marines. Not only is the book world of the Thirties—which accorded him a respectable spot off to one side from its more typical social indignants—a long way behind us, but Thomason in essence was a long way behind the Thirties, his impulses not forward toward the changes the reformists sternly sought, but backward beyond changes that had already taken place. Industrially massive and sophisticated techniques of slaughter and a waning of the sense of imperial mission have wrecked most moderns' appreciation of the virtues of old-fashioned good soldiering, and the general idea of the Southern ethos these days seems to be summed up in *Life* photographs of pussel-gutted Cotton Belt sheriffs secure in tyranny. In a forward-plunging world, retrospective writers tend to lose their place in the sun rather quickly, unless their writing has such excellence that no one can ignore it, like the poetry of Yeats.

Most of Thomason's writing has sizable defects that shut it off from that sort of excellence. A lot of it came out first in periodicals, often the big popular magazines which in those days satisfied the mass middle-class appetite for affirmation that feeds today on television. In consequence a good number—possibly most—of Thomason's story plots are more or less afflicted with a hollow slickness that is out of O. Henry by way of George Horace Lorimer of the old *Saturday Evening Post*. These plots are by nature sentimental, putting pat wishful rightness ahead of esthetic or philosophic rightness, and they often breed further sentimentality in the characterizations and the very style of a writer whose deepest perceptions were not sentimental at all, but ironic or tragic. Nor is the trouble restricted to his stories published in such magazines, for that kind of thing can rub off onto other work if it gets to be a habit. Even Thomason's rich sense of the world's textures—of country and weather and creatures and human thrust and laughter and history—is frequently infected and diminished by it, as in his only novel, *Gone to Texas*.

Yet a writer merits being judged on the best work he has done, and Thomason's best still seems to me to be distinctive and good, whether it is fashionable or not just now. He never found a right form for his fiction. His finest book, *Lone Star Preacher*, is an assemblage of Civil War tales and anecdotes given loose unity by its focus on a main character, the Reverend Praxiteles Swan, who set gentleness for a time aside and served the God of Battles in Hood's Texas Brigade. But despite this casual shape, it has sustained descriptions of fighting that in their distinctive way are quite as starkly moving as anything in Stephen Crane or other noted scribes of war, and with a spare powerful prose it manipulates the themes of the doomed Southern Rebellion and soldiering's grim dignity to build a feeling of the whole tragic worthwhileness of mortal endeavor:

The two, in the sleety night, found nothing to say to each other. They thought they might as well go back to the command. They got their horses from the livery stable. The sleet had changed to a wet snow, driven on a bitter wind.

The widely spaced street lights were blanketed, and made luminous yellow spheres of radiance, that gave no light at all. The horses' hooves were muffled on the road. They seemed, to themselves, riding with their heads bent against the wind, the last lonely souls in a world of cold and sleep.

They came to a crossroads where all directions looked the same. "Which road, Elder, which road?" asked Major Martin impatiently. "I'm kind of turned around."

Praxiteles lifted his beard from his chest and answered, out of a dark dream. "Either road will take us where we're going. It don't matter now—Same distance and no choice—"

Off to the west and south the rain was falling through the naked boughs of tall trees that stood gaunt around a place called Appomattox.

I think it is not necessary to have had Mr. Frank Dobie take the book down from his shelf and read that passage and a few others aloud to you in his own Old Breed accent, as he did for me once, to know that it is a cut above just good writing and that it bespeaks more than a minor talent. It came in Thomason's latter years, a culmination of his better prose efforts. If he had lived for a few years past the age of fifty-one, he might have done much more that good or better still.

His drawings generally share the same themes, the Old Breed themes, of the writing to which so many of them are tied, but on the whole they handle the themes better. Few are sentimental or "cute" in the manner of some of Thomason's less felicitous fiction, and those few are so because they directly portray cute or sentimental fictional situations. Most of the rest can stand strongly alone, independent of the writing. Many, for that matter, are only contrapuntally related to the printed material with which they were published. Throughout his life Thomason was an obsessed sketcher, pausing in battle, in Latin-American jungles, on ships, in the hunting field, and along the side streets and waterfronts and market squares of the world to make quick and accurate drawings of people and things that caught his eye, and often he used these later as illustrations for writing, good or indifferent, whose theme or locale coincided with theirs.

Almost from the start his drawings possessed a certainty and a rightness that are found only fitfully in most of his fiction. They are frankly and superbly representational, rich with the feelings that Thomason had about their subjects, though seldom weighted or twisted toward those feelings' expression. They have a lean tough exactness about them, a line or a slash or a dot often conveying the precise shade of fear or benevolence or false dignity or berserker combat rage that the artist was after, and the sureness and loving authenticity of their details reflect the passion with which he cared about physical existence, and about the way history's messages loom in the aspect of men and things. When you look at sketches he did of Mangin's dire Senegalese, whom he had seen in action, and of Rebel foot soldiers and Napoleonic hussars, whom he had not, you know that that is the way those men looked, in dress, in equipment, and in essence. And though you may have burned your draft card in front of ten thousand folks to flaunt your abhorrence of war, you know also that those men's essence is very anciently and proudly human and very deadly, and that it has a great beauty of its own regardless of whether you like it or even whether it is on your side of the fence in a given fight.

For these things were a part of Thomason's special

soldierly understanding. He knew uniquely and intimately how to feel that sort of men, and he know how to get his feeling across without beating it into you with a hammer. He felt other things too, and communicated them. More than all but the absolute best of his writing, his drawings hold strongly his own personal flavor—interested, thoughtful, often ironic but just as often compassionate, leaning toward a concern with male forcefulness and its trappings and consequences but alert also to the lovely cant of a floozie's tail and the five thousand years' woe that shaped the shoulders of a Chinese peasant.

In abstract matters of form and composition, I am told by persons who know more than I do about such analysis that Thomason's graphic work, at least in those items that are not just fragments, comes amply up to snuff. These persons sometimes add, though, that it is a shame he gave himself so little scope, for the bulk of what he did was black-and-white and swift in execution, hence limited in its potential for subtlety and depth and broad meaning. I am sure this must be so, for it is paralleled by roughly similar limitations in his writing; in both media he tended toward sketches rather than fuller forms. Maybe it came partly from his having fitted his creative work into the spare time of a military career, or maybe not . . . Whatever its origins, it is not something that is going to be changed now, and I believe that the main question worth asking, with the Colonel a quarter-century under the sod at Huntsville, where he had been born into an organic if imperfect Old Breed world, is whether it matters in human terms that he made his drawings at all, and wrote his tales and stories.

Admitting to a probable want of objectivity, I think it does matter, solidly. Ours is a loud and urgent and changeful age, full of ephemeral self-expression and trivial bombast, hot for novelty, hell-bent on moving forward into an uncertain and possibly catastrophic future. We are little addicted to looking back—perhaps because, as Satchel Paige said, something might be gaining on us. But the chances are that the kind of people who will walk here more calmly later, after the uproar subsides, will not have been so changed as to lose their sense of kinship with the whole draggled magnificent train of humanity that preceded them on the crust of this planet, and that like the inhabitants of other calm ages they will seek fuller understanding of themselves through scrutiny of the past.

And when they do pause and look back to see where they came from, their main understandings will derive from the creations of artists of various kinds, major and minor, who like John Thomason in his best work saw certain of life's meanings and textures clearly and set them down right. After all the ephemeral self-expression and bombast and marred insights of any age have turned to dust or mist and blown away, what is left is the work of such people. There is never enough of it, and it matters very much.

CONTENTS

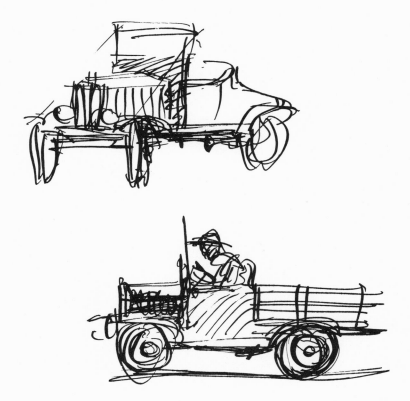

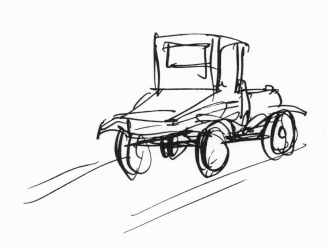

A THOMASON SKETCHBOOK

Bayou Teche

Glimpses of Home

drowned field

Mallards –
Jan 1916

A War Long Ago

"Their fiah come down the hill in blizzards—you could lean against it. A fellow could'a swung a quart cup an' caught a peck of minies in it. That was bad and the rocks an' the bushes was bad—and some mighty strong Yankees on top of all—No, seh, no, seh. Godalmighty didn't mean us to take that hill—" so they said in Texas long afterwards. But Praxiteles began to chant, in the flame and fury of it:

"Come on, Fifth Texas,
  Come on, Fifth Texians—
  You boys from the Brazos
  And the Trinity
  From the Colorado, and from
  Buffalo Bayou.
  From Corpus Christi
  and Galveston—
  Come on, you Texicans,
  Remember Gaines's Mill where you broke them
  and drove them—
  Remember Freeman's Ford—
  Remember Groveton.
  Remember 2d Manasas, where
  you killed the Fire Zouaves—
  —Remember Sharpsburg
  Where the Lord of Hosts was on our side and
  the legions of hell
  could not prevail against us—
  Remember Fredericksburg
  Where they stood in rows like corn under the sun—

(blast and confound you to everlastin' Hell-fire Joe Ruggers, don't shoot blind over that rock—)

Remember all your battles and marches . . .
Come on, Fifth Texas . . ."

—John W. Thomason, Jr.
Lone Star Preacher

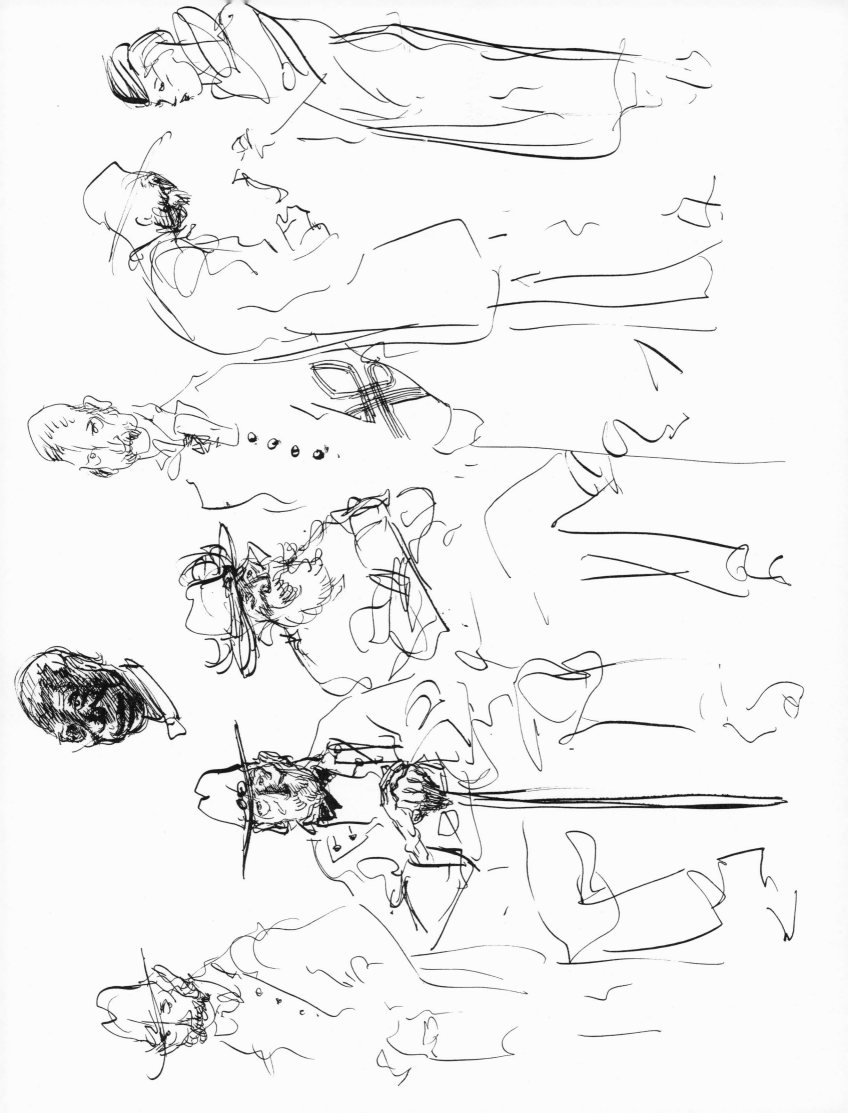

A Few Marines

N. M. C. 161
400m-64-DQMPa—7-28-19

UNITED STATES MARINE CORPS

MARINE BARRACKS

"Target: 'eator at 12 o'clock: range: battle-sight! ———"

S' man wantosis.
Rendova

80

The Marine Abroad

They relate of Charles the Second that at Whitehall a certain sea-captain, newly-returned from the Western Ocean, told the king of flying fish, a thing never heard in Old England. The king and the court were vastly amused. But, the naval fellow persisting, the Merry Monarch beckoned to a lean, dry colonel of the sea regiment, with a seamed mahogany face, and said, in effect: "Colonel, this tarry-breeks here makes sport with us stay-at-homes. He tells of a miraculous fish that forsakes its element and flies like a bird over the water!" "Sire," said the colonel of Marines, "he tells a true thing. I myself have often seen those fish in your Majesty's seas around Barbados—" "Well," decided Charles, "such evidence cannot be disputed. And hereafter, when we hear a strange thing, we will tell it to the Marines, for the Marines go everywhere and see everything, and if they say it is so, we will believe it!"

—John W. Thomason, Jr.
Fix Bayonets!

Japanese Bluejacket patrol Chapei.

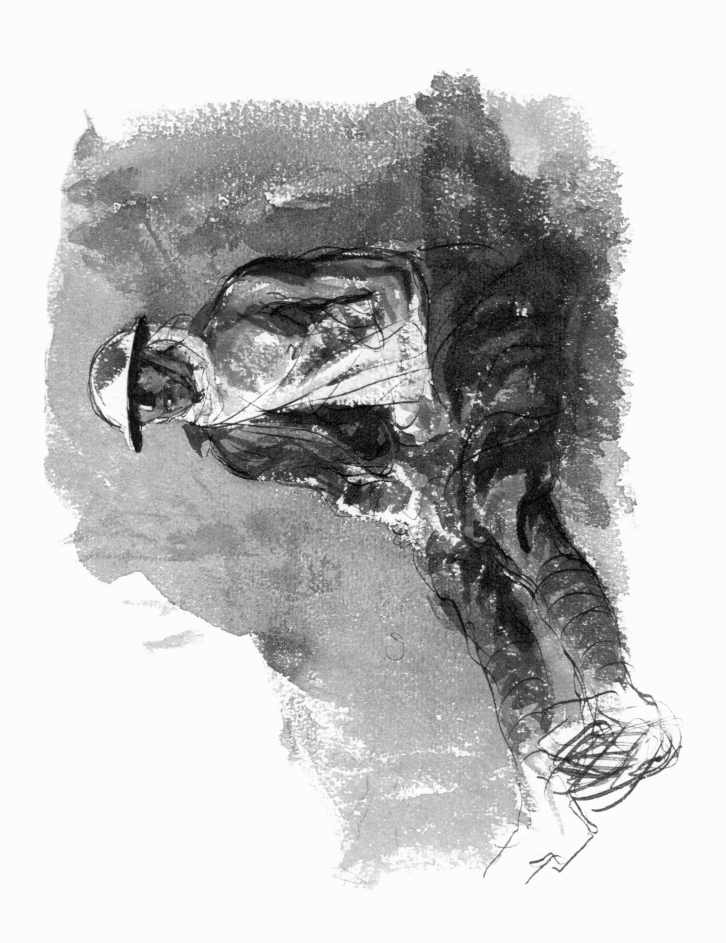

This is a more refined
type than average + I tried
to get a more typical soldier
to pose, but Col. Aihara, the
commandant personally
selected this fellow and I
had to take him —

Corporal of the Japanese Guard. Peking 1932

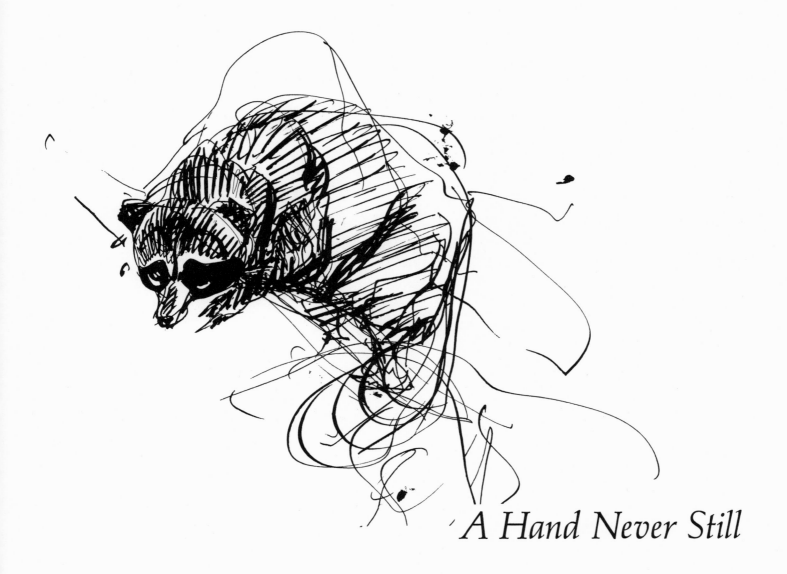

A Hand Never Still

In pen, pencil, or water color, the free stroke conveying movement and life, which is the mark of the artist born, was always his . . . [Thomason] seemed born with the craft of writing and drawing both at his fingertips.

—William Rose Benet
Saturday Review of Literature
(March, 1944)

Presumably an embassy reception. The lean young officer at the left is a self-portrait of John Thomason.

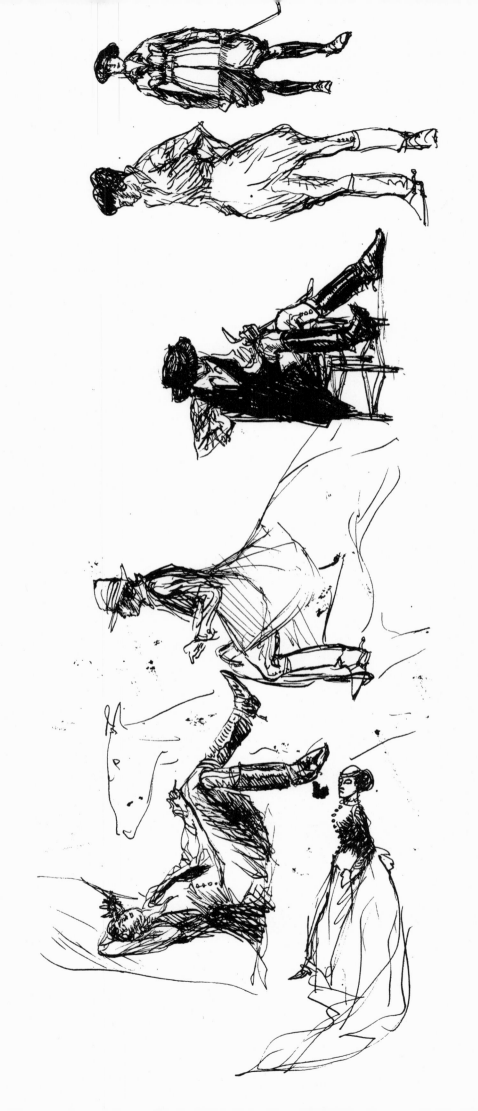

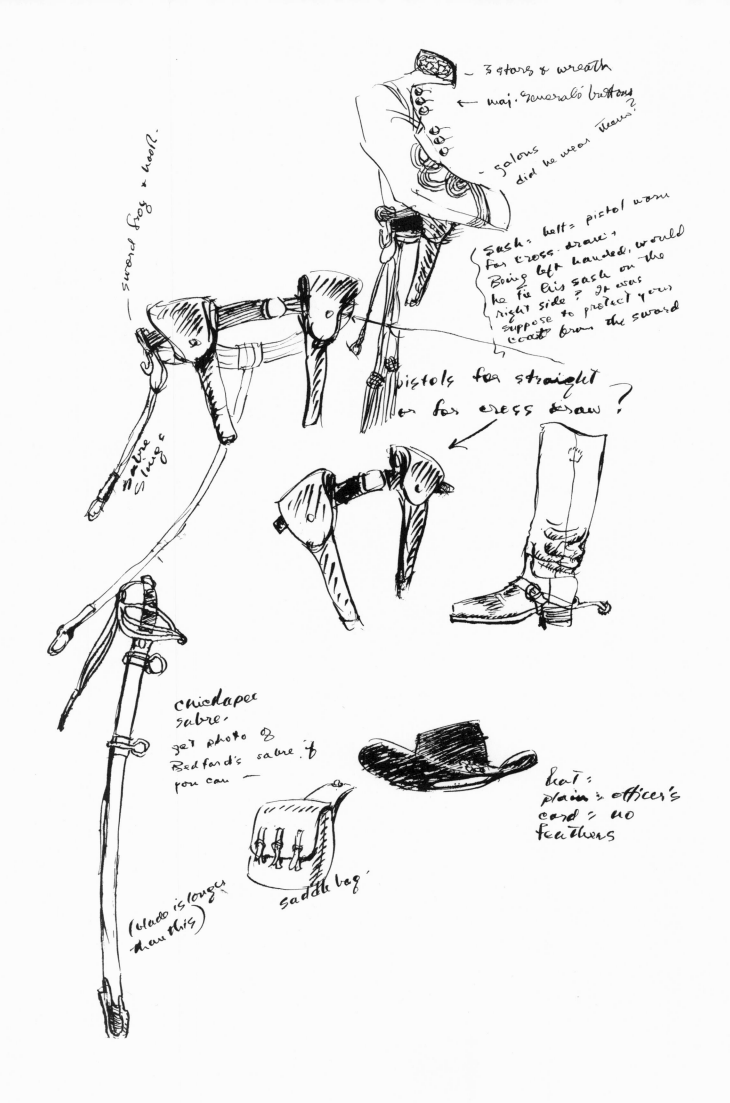

- 3 stars & wreath
- maj. generals buttons
- galons — did he wear them?

sash: belt = pistol worn
for cross draw.
Being left handed, would
he tie his sash on the
right side? It was
suppose to protect your
coat from the sword

pistols for straight
or for cross draw?

Sword Frog & hook.

Sabre Sling

chicdaper
sabre.
get photo of
Bedford's sabre if
you can —

(blade is longer
than this)

saddle bag

hat:
plain : officer's
cord : no
feathers

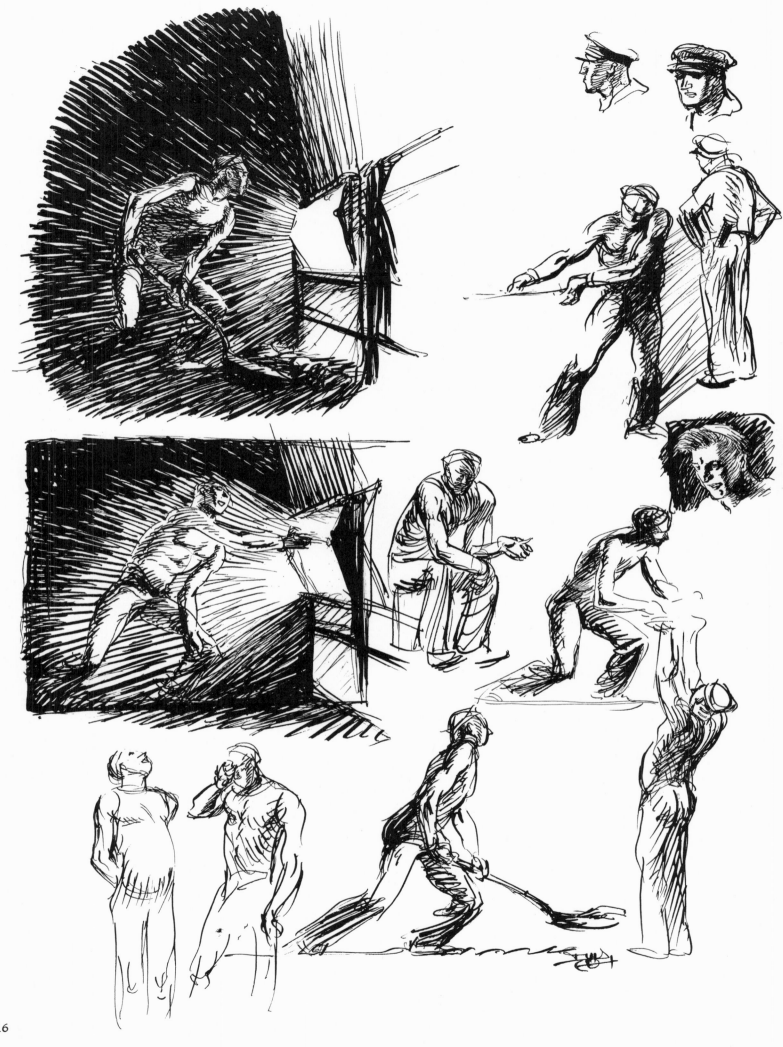

116

118

Four preliminary sketches for an illustration for Thomason's edition of *Adventures of General Marbot*. Fifth in series is the completed illustration (page 123).

Corporal of the Regiment
of mounted Rifles. 1855

127